Chicago Public Library
Humboldt Park Branch
1605 N. Troy Street
Chicago, IL 60647
(312) 744 - 2244